# CRAZY CREATURES

# The FACT ATTACK series

Awesome Aliens
Beastly Bodies
Cool Cars
Crazy Creatures
Crucial Cricket
Dastardly Deeds
Deadly Deep
Devastating Dinosaurs
Dreadful Disasters
Fantastic Football
Gruesome Ghosts
Incredible Inventions
Mad Medicine
Magnificent Monarchs
Nutty Numbers
Remarkable Rescues
Rowdy Rugby
Spectacular Space
Super Spies
Vile Vampires

# FACT ATTACK

# CRAZY CREATURES

# IAN LOCKE

MACMILLAN CHILDREN'S BOOKS

First published 1998 by Macmillan Children's Books

This edition published 2012 by Macmillan Children's Books
a division of Macmillan Publishers Limited
20 New Wharf Road, London N1 9RR
Basingstoke and Oxford
Associated companies throughout the world
www.panmacmillan.com

ISBN 978-1-4472-2417-4

1 3 5 7 9 8 6 4 2

A CIP catalogue record for this book is available from
the British Library.

Printed and bound by CPI Group (UK) Ltd, Croydon CR0 4YY

# DID YOU KNOW THAT . . .

 The giant squid is one of the longest creatures on earth – it can grow up to 15 metres or 45 foot. It also has the largest eyes of any living animal; they are up to 38 cm across.

 A female elephant will always adopt a baby elephant which has lost its mother.

Evelyn Françon of France found his cat Graffiti messy and noisy and gave him away to friends 100 miles away when he moved to a new job in 1995. A few months later his friends told him that Graffiti had run away. In January 1997 Evelyn heard a scratching and screeching at his front door. It was Graffiti! The cat had spent two years making the journey through the foothills of the French Alps to his old owner's new home in Isère. Evelyn said, "I shall have to keep him now."

 A dog's sense of smell can be amazing. A Doberman once tracked a sheep thief for 100 miles by scent alone across the Great Karoo plain in South Africa.

 There are 30 species of slug in Britain.

When he moved to Italy, the British artist and writer Edward Lear, famous for his nonsense rhymes, built a new house. The house was exactly the same as the one he had lived in in Britain so his cat would feel at home.

 The rattlesnake or viper has special cells between its nostril and its eye. These are sensitive to infrared radiant heat and can locate people in the dark by the heat they give off.

In June 1986 Blackie, a 3 kg Siamese cat, was minding his own business in his garden in Droxford, Hampshire, when a dark shadow appeared overhead. In moments a buzzard swooped down, picked up Blackie in its claws and flew off. Blackie hissed and struggled so much that the bird dropped him back into the garden. Though the 'cat-nap' lasted only a minute or two, Blackie was lucky. Buzzards normally kill their prey before flying off with it.

 The male emperor penguin looks after the egg of its young for between 105 and 115 days in a temperature of about -16°C. During this time it has nothing to eat and only survives by huddling together with other males on ice floes.

 In February 1996 an Australian scientist put a lawnmower powered by rabbits on show.

Shayne, the world's oldest horse, is 51 years old! He lives at a sanctuary in Brentford, Essex.

 48 rats were on the space shuttle Columbia in 1993.

 The average lifespan of a robin is 18 months.

 At Felpham in England, the owner of a white Samoyed dog made socks, scarves, gloves and jumpers from the dog's hair. After the film *101 Dalmatians* was released in the USA, there was a craze for clothes made from dog hair. Dog fur was made into overcoats in Mongolia in 1996.

So many starlings settled on the minute hand of Big Ben one day in 1945 that it was slowed by 5 minutes.

 The polar bear's nose is the only part of its body not covered in fur. When at rest, the bear covers its nose to keep it warm and help heat the air it is breathing. The bear's fur is translucent, and seems white because of the light passing through it. While polar bears can live in very cold areas, they seem to like a temperature of between 10 and 15°C most.

 The second busiest stock market in America, called the NASDAQ, was closed on 16 August 1994 when a squirrel chewed the power lines to the main computer.

During the filming of an episode of *Baywatch* near Los Angeles, star David Hasselhoff helped save the victim of an attack by an alligator being used in the episode.

 A St Bernard dog had a record litter of 15 puppies in October 1993 in Taunton, Somerset.

 The first society to stop cruelty to animals was begun in London in 1824. One of those involved was William Wilberforce, the man who also stopped the slave trade.

 The fastest growing creature on Earth is the blue whale. From the time it begins growing to full growth it increases up to 30,000 million times in size.

The giant megamouth shark was discovered by the US Navy in 1976.

Any type of rabbit can be a pet. Among the names of types of rabbits are Rex, British Giant, Dwarf Lop and Netherland Dwarf. A British Giant rabbit can grow to twice the size of a fully grown cat and weigh up to 12 kg.

In Roman times, the poet Virgil once held a funeral for a fly. The funeral cost about £50,000!

The tallest animal on earth is the giraffe. It can grow up to 6 metres high.

Among the animals seen around Britain which are not native to the country were a South American parakeet caught in Scotland in 1895, a European wolf in 1904, a jackal in Kent in 1905 and a lynx in the Highlands of Scotland in 1927.

 In 1948 a cat named Mincha climbed up a 12-metre tree in Buenos Aires, Argentina. She did not want to come down and was still there in 1954. Her food was sent up by pole and she had at least three lots of kittens while in the tree, without coming down!

 If they need to, many cats can climb straight up. In 1980 a cat frightened by a dog in Bradford climbed 20 metres up the straight wall of a block of flats.

In South Africa in 1937 a miner reported finding a worm 7 metres long, which left a tunnel 3 cm across.

 The ghost bat of Australia is a cannibal.

 The Endangered Species Act was passed in the USA in 1973. It helped to protect animals from hunters and to stop the destruction of the environment.

In 1995, a four-year-old black and white terrier dog, Rosie, ran away from her home near Colchester on Christmas afternoon. After a search lasting 72 hours, Rosie's owner heard her. She was trapped in an underground drain. The entrance was too small for a person to get down. Knowing the danger that Rosie was in, her owner contacted a rescue club. They decided to use a trained rescue dog, a terrier named Vic. Vic was given an electronic bleeper for his collar and sent down into the dark, freezing pipe in search of Rosie. Vic found where Rosie was stuck, and stopped there. The workmen waiting above then dug down the two metres to the pipe. The pipe was then smashed with an axe and the two dogs scampered out into the light. Rosie was thin, dirty and hungry, but otherwise unharmed. She went home to a huge meal and the new collar she had been given for Christmas.

The story of *101 Dalmatians*, by the British writer Dodie Smith, was based on her own dogs. The first Dalmatian she had she decided to call Pongo. When Pongo had pups, she began to think about a story about Dalmatians.

 The only poisonous bird is the orange and black songbird, the hooded Pitohui, discovered by accident in New Guinea in 1992.

 Charles Cruft, who started the famous Cruft's dog shows in London, never owned a dog and never went to his shows. He had a pet cat.

 The average caterpillar has 16 legs.

The first cat working for the Post Office, to catch mice, arrived in London in 1868. The cats which were used by the Post Office in Britain were paid "a shilling [5p] a week and all the mice you can catch". By 1983 the pay of cats was £2 a week.

 Sharks have killed more people in Australia than anywhere else in the world. The number killed is not huge – only a few hundred since 1791.

Some dogs can become very attached to their masters. Among the strangest stories of such closeness is that of Susie, a fox terrier owned by Lord Carnarvon. Lord Carnarvon, who put up the money for the finding of the tomb of Tutankhamun in Egypt, was dying in Cairo, the capital of Egypt. He had blood poisoning from an infected mosquito bite. Back in England, at his stately home of Highclere, Susie went downstairs and fell dead in the hall. It was exactly the same time that her master died. Why or how this happened no one can explain.

 If a cow eats snakeroot, a poisonous plant, the poison goes into the milk. The mother of the famous American president, Lincoln, died after drinking milk infected by this poison.

The elephant is the only animal with four knees.

 The blue whale can grow up to over 30 metres long and weigh over 100 tonnes. It is the longest and heaviest animal ever known to have lived. The female is larger than the male. They can eat up to about 1,000 kg of the plankton krill at one time. When born, the baby blue whale, called a calf, is about 7 metres long.

 The average woodpecker pecks 20 times a second.

The King of Thailand, King Bhumibol, has 11 white elephants in his animal collection. Long ago the King of Siam, as Thailand was then called, would present one of the sacred white elephants to anyone he particularly disliked. As a royal animal, the elephant could not be used for work, so it could not work in the quarries or in the forests, so the owner had to pay to keep the elephant. This was so expensive that it led to the expression "a white elephant" for anything which has to be kept at great expense but has no use.

 The biggest bird known to have lived in recent times is the Madagascan elephant bird which died out 300 years ago, in about 1660. Its egg was 30 cm large and could hold 7 litres. It was also known as the "Roc bird", was about 3 metres high and weighed nearly 500 kg. The name of the bird was used in the *Tales of Sinbad*.

A bite from a black mamba snake, which can grow up to 4 metres long, nearly always kills a person. The snake lives in south and central Africa. When the snake bites, a person will feel dizzy, then find it difficult to breathe, then the heart beats erratically until the person dies.

 Male elephants can get drunk. They will eat unripe millet and then become drunk. When drunk they will start dancing, teasing each other and falling over. The male elephants make sure that female and young elephants do not eat the millet.

 The only place in the world where dolphins regularly live close to people is at Monkey Mia, on the coast of western Australia.

Some types of ants eat wood. At one time ants ate a railway! It was the wooden railway which ran from Singapore through to Thailand in Asia. In 1877 the ants chomped their way through tons of wooden sleepers and rails until there was nothing left of the track. The railway was rebuilt in steel and concrete.

 Baby rabbits are known as kittens. In old times, sailors thought rabbits were unlucky so they never used the word "rabbit", giving them names or calling them "thing" instead.

A monkey called Johnny learned to drive a tractor on a sheep farm near Melbourne, Australia. Johnny began just as a pet of the farm's owner, but soon learned to open and shut gates after copying his master. When he learned to drive the tractor he somehow knew that it had to be started in neutral. Johnny drove the tractor in a straight line or along a path on signals and calls from his owner. At lunchtime the monkey had his own lunchbag, putting the litter back in the bag after he'd finished.

 The ringhals or spitting cobra snake spits venom through holes in its front fangs or teeth. If the venom hits a person's eyes it can cause blindness.

The world's most travelled cat is probably a three-year-old tabby called Tabitha, owned by American actress Carol Timmel. In 1995 Tabitha escaped from her carrier when she was in a jumbo jet flying across America. After a search she could not be found. Over the next 12 days the jumbo continued to fly back and forth across America. During this time Tabitha's owner decided that the airline, Tower Air, had not made a proper search for her pet. So, when the jumbo landed, a second search for Tabitha was made. She was eventually found hiding behind a passenger compartment. Apart from being dirty, she was fine. No one was admitting what she might have eaten during her 12 days' journey. The total number of miles she flew while wandering the plane was over 30,000!

 By the time the dog film star Rin Tin Tin died aged 16 in Hollywood in 1932, he had a butler, a personal cook and a car which took him to the film set!

The tarantula spider is said to be dangerous, but its bite is really harmless; at worst it causes only a little swelling and some pain.

 About every four years the number of lemmings (furry creatures related to squirrels) in a group grows quickly. If there is not enough food, large numbers of the animals move and spread out. They will cross mountains, walls, cliffs and even try to cross the sea when they move in large numbers like this. Many die when they go on the march in this way; it is a type of mass suicide. What makes the lemmings stop moving is not clear.

 Owls stay quiet when they fly because they have feathers on their feet.

Elephants can catch a cold, but they do not sneeze very often.

 A tortoise can live for up to 200 years; by contrast the usual lifespan of a hamster is only four years. A tortoise which died in 1966 was 188 years old. It was presented to the King of Tonga in 1773 by Captain Cook.

 Rats cannot vomit.

 The sea otter never gets its skin wet when it goes in the sea. It has two coats of fur, which keep its skin perfectly dry.

 Emperor Napoleon of France was terrified by cats.

In 1987 five-year-old Carlton Carroll was knocked out by a brown spotted stingray fish which leaped into the family fishing boat when he was out with his family off the coast of America.

 Wild ducks can get flu.

 The dog that bites the least is a golden retriever.

 The first guide dogs were used in Germany in a home for blind people, in 1916. The first ever guide dog was called Excelsior. He was trained by a Doctor Gorlitz to lead a blind man across the lawn. After this worked, guide dogs were used all over Germany, then all over the world.

 The tongue of a chameleon is hollow.

Judy, an English dog, was a hero during the Second World War. She was born in the city of Shanghai in China. She was looked after by men of the British Royal Navy aboard a gunboat. One day the gunboat was torpedoed by the Japanese Navy. Judy and some of the men were taken prisoner. She spent two years in a Japanese prison camp on the island of Sumatra. Her owners were used as slaves by the Japanese to build a railway. During the time she was a prisoner Judy attacked the Japanese guards and helped prisoners who were about to be beaten. In 1945 she and her fellow prisoners were rescued and released.

A mother cat, Scarlett, became a heroine in Brooklyn, New York, in April 1996. A fire broke out in an abandoned building. Several floors up, the stray Scarlett began to rescue all her five kittens, one by one. In and out she went. She carried each of them down in her mouth, made sure they were all right and went back into the fire. Each time her red fur got more burned and her eyes were seared by the heat. Finally she got the last of her kittens out. She stood guard over them until they were all rescued by firemen. Scarlett and her kittens all recovered. Hundreds of people heard the story and wanted to look after Scarlett and the kittens.

 A fly's taste buds are in its feet.

Lesley Kelly, who was born blind, has an unusual guide dog – a poodle called Valda. Lesley had tried two other kinds of guide dogs – a Labrador and a retriever. But the Labrador was too fast for her and the retriever too slow. Valda was just right.

 An alligator can swallow a 4 kg chicken in one gulp.

 When on land, otters use their tail as a third leg to stand up, strut across the ground or peer over objects in their path. When underwater, small flaps on their ears close up so they do not get water in them.

A cat has a normal body temperature of 38.6°C. A dog's average temperature is 38.3°C. A human's is 37°C.

 In Hong Kong, where the older buildings are very close together, a man was once killed by a falling pig. The pig had fallen from a balcony. The story was so strange that the British writer Graham Greene wrote about it. His story was turned into a short film in the 1980s, which won an Oscar. It was not the only time such a thing happened. In 1987 Lui Wai-Kwong, aged 36, was injured when he was hit on the head by a one-kilogram turtle which fell on him as he walked to work. Again the turtle must have fallen from the balcony of a building above him.

 An ostrich's intestines are up to 15 metres long.

Ostrich chicks grow about 1.5 metres in their first year.

 Elephants eat for about 18 hours a day.

 Bats can get too hot and get heat-stroke. Thousands of bats were affected by the heat in Fort Worth, Texas, USA, in 1989. They fell out of the sky on to buildings and into the busy streets.

 The black rat brought the bubonic plague to Europe.

 A cow's sweat glands are in its nose. Cow's noses are like human fingerprints – they can be used to identify the cow.

The tongue of the Australian platypus has teeth. It eats its own weight in worms every day.

 The okapi is one of the world's strangest animals. It has eyes that can look both ways at the same time, a see-through tongue which is up to 35 cm long, and four stomachs. It has the legs of a zebra, the body of an antelope, the walk of a giraffe, the speed of an ostrich and the courage of a tiger. They spend almost all their lives on their own.

 Flies can get athlete's foot.

 Caves in New Zealand are lit by glow-worms.

Almost all smaller cats hate to get soaking wet. One sort which does not is the Turkish van cat, which can swim well. They also like playing in the rain. Other cats can swim, even if they don't like it. In the 1997 floods in America many cats were forced to swim for their lives.

 One scrambled ostrich egg will feed six people for breakfast.

 Pigs have up to 44 teeth.

 The turkey was given its name by the British. The French called this American bird the Indian bird. In Turkey they are called "American birds".

 A temple devoted to the worship of rats was built in the village of Deshnok, India.

The live-action version of *101 Dalmatians* used over 400 animals, 220 of them Dalmatian puppies. All the 220 puppies were born and lived in England because pets are not allowed to come into Britain without first going into quarantine for six months. Some of the puppies used in the film were "made" on a computer and then fitted into the "real" live-action film.

The thick hairs on ants' legs are used as combs. They often groom each other with them. Ants also keep pets; they are very fond of keeping a type of cricket in their burrows in winter.

The first turtle was brought to London in 1752 by Admiral Anson. Turtles and tortoises cannot move their ribs, so they breathe by pushing air through their necks. Turtles' necks have an extra water supply.

In the nineteenth century a clergyman in England found a brown rat in his house. The rat soon became a pet and quite tame. One night the man was woken up by the rat biting his cheek. Looking around he found to his alarm that the curtains on his four-poster bed were on fire. The man quickly made his way out of the house, which was burned to the ground. Unfortunately he was never to see his heroic pet again.

The honeybee is the only bee that dies after stinging a person or object.

Hannibal, the general who led the army of the city of Carthage against the Romans almost two thousand years ago, became famous for crossing the Alps. In his army he had 90,000 soldiers on foot, 12,000 cavalry and 37 elephants. The poor elephants were not suited to the cold and length of this journey into Italy. Only one of them is supposed to have survived.

The only mammal that can fly is the bat.

 The eggs of a green turtle, which look like ping-pong balls, bounce.

 The lesser rorqual whale, which can grow to 11 metres long, seems to like playing near ships. It has often been seen by sailors jumping out of the sea, sometimes lying on its back!

 The bee is the only insect that produces food eaten by man.

 When snow once closed the border between France and Switzerland, a Swiss circus decided the animals could go over the border on foot. The elephants, dogs and horses all went for their walk. The monkeys didn't – they were nervous of the snow. They were taken by taxi!

Baby chickens can live three days after they hatch without eating.

 The great horned owl is the only animal that will eat skunk.

 The kiwi is the only bird that has nostrils at the end of its bill.

 The ancient Egyptian army was once defeated by cats! The King of Persia came up with a plan. He sent soldiers with cats in their arms at the head of his army. The Egyptians, who treated cats as gods and did not dare harm them, surrendered.

 Jaguars are scared of dogs.

In Oregon, in the United States, a kitten became friends with a 250 kg grizzly bear at a wildlife park. When the starving kitten first arrived, in 1995, the grizzly took out a piece of chicken from its food bucket and gave it to the hungry kitten.

 Shrews have two sorts of sounds – they twitter and scream. They only scream when they meet another shrew.

 You can preserve unrefrigerated ground camel meat with garlic.

 As soon as a bat hangs upside down, it becomes colder. Bats have five fingers, which are part of each wing; they also have five toes and ankles. The long-eared bats fold their big ears along their bodies when they go to sleep and cover them with their wings.

Hares live out in the open in a small dip they make in the ground, which is called a "form".

 There are more chickens than people in the world.

 Manx cats of the Isle of Man have no tails.

 The Siamese cat is almost white when born. Their brown colour appears as they grow. They only have dark or black colours on the parts of their body which are cold. If Siamese cats are left in the cold too long, their coats will turn darker and darker.

In London in the 1950s, Mr Henry Cooper liked to play darts. His dog Ace liked to help him! Ace would collect the darts from the board and give them back to the players. To get the darts at the top of the board, Ace would jump two metres into the air!

 Squirrels, beavers and other rodents have very sharp teeth. The reason why their teeth are so sharp is that they have protecting enamel only on the front part of their teeth. As they use their teeth, the backs get worn down so the teeth become sharper and sharper.

 A flamingo can only eat when its head is upside down.

 Packs of wolves travel up to 50 miles from their lairs in their search for food. When they move, they always try and keep to a straight line, moving at a trot.

African elephants stay on their feet for 30 or 40 years.

 The dolphin can swim at up to 24 miles an hour.

 Ship's cats are good swimmers. Early in their lives they fall or are knocked into the sea and get used to water. They do not seem bothered by the salt in the sea.

 A hummingbird cannot stand on its own two feet; they are not strong enough to hold up the bird on a flat surface. The bill of the swordbill hummingbird is longer than its body.

Barry was a giant St Bernard dog who lived in the mountains of Switzerland in the early 1800s. He was looked after by monks, who went out to guide people across the mountains and help rescue them if they were in trouble. Barry somehow knew when bad weather was coming. He would lead the monks out to the people trapped in the bad weather or under the snow of an avalanche. He helped rescue 40 people. He became so famous that when he died, his body was kept. It can still be seen in a museum in Switzerland. In Paris, France, a giant statue of Barry was put up in the dog cemetery there. Not all St Bernards are heroic. On Boxing Day in 1996 a St Bernard called Freddie had to be cut free by firemen from a cat flap. He got his head stuck in it after chasing after a cat in Basingstoke, Hampshire.

 The European oyster starts its life as a male, then changes into a female.

Cats pull at furniture and carpets to get rid of old claws, not to sharpen them.

 14% of Dalmatians are completely deaf. The young Dalmatian will only begin to hear at about 6 weeks.

 The ancient Egyptians shaved off their eyebrows to mourn the death of their cats.

 When food was in short supply in Germany after the Second World War, the grass-eating animals at one zoo were let out to feed in the local town parks, squares and playgrounds.

The death's head moth will fly up to 3,000 miles each year from Africa to Europe. During the war they sometimes landed on ships in the Atlantic, happy to find a spot to rest for the day.

 A cod lays up to 9 million eggs, a salmon lays only 10–20,000. Sharks lay the largest eggs – almost 15 cm long. The pods of the eggs are baked brown by the sun.

 A dog's heart beats 40 times a minute faster than a human's.

 In a local cricket match in Bedfordshire in 1955, a player hit the ball into a field. It was eaten by a cow called Bessie. The game was then abandoned, as the club did not have another cricket ball. Bessie seemed fine.

Tuna fish swim at an average speed of 9 miles an hour all the time; they never stop moving.

 Ant colonies have doctors. Sick ants are isolated. If they are too injured, they are killed off.

 Ants seem to have monthly holidays when they do nothing.

 Ants will sleep about three hours a day.

 A domestic (pet) cat has 18 claws, five on both of the front paws and four on the back paws.

The milk of sheep, goats and cows can be used to make cheese. The French cheese Roquefort comes from sheep at a place called Larzac. These sheep never drink water. The shepherds believe that if the sheep drink water their wool will become less soft and their meat less tender.

 Snakes cannot cry. They do not have eyelids. Instead their eyes are protected by a clear skin.

 At night crocodiles can be stunned by artificial lights. Their eyes reflect a red colour and they stay very still. Crocodiles have a semi-transparent third eyelid which slides over their eyes when they are underwater.

The star-nosed mole swims well, has fur like an otter and lives on the edge of swamps in America. In very dry weather it can die of thirst.

 Only half the world's spiders spin webs; the rest of them hunt for their food. The largest web is spun by the tropical golden-orb web spider. Its web can be up to 1.5 m across and held up by lines up to 6 m long. The smallest web is made by the midget spider, less than 12 mm across. The web of a garden spider can have up to 30 m of strong silk; this silk can be stretched six times its length without breaking then return to normal size. It is stronger than steel.

 Earthworms have five hearts.

 The only domestic animal not mentioned in the Bible is the cat.

The male mosquito does not bite – only the female does. They also prefer to bite people who are blond.

A female African elephant carries her baby for 22 months before it is born.

Sheep in Iceland eat seaweed during the long, cold winter.

Cats in Edwardsville, Illinois, in the USA, have to wear a bell by law.

Bees build their home from top to bottom. A swarm of bees weighs about 2.5 kg. Inside the hive, even in winter, they try to keep the temperature at about 24°C. When the temperature goes below this, the bees begin to beat their wings and the warmth of their bodies heats up the hive. When they are making wax the temperature of the hive can reach 36°C and just before they swarm, it can be up to 40°C.

 Because of an early winter in the Alps, the airline Swiss Air flew 200,000 swallows across the mountains in 1974.

 A baby crocodile once hatched out in a lawyer's office in South Africa. The lawyer had been given the egg by a friend, had wrapped it in old socks and put it on a shelf with old books. Nearly three weeks later, out came the 20 cm baby croc!

A cow can give 400 pints (227 litres) of milk a week.

 The world's biggest clams weigh over 200 kg.

 Camels from Tibet were used for ploughing on Russian farms during the Second World War.

 The Tokyo zoo in Japan is closed for two months a year, so the animals can have a holiday from the visitors.

 Seals have been known to swim for as long as 8 months and as far as 6,000 miles without touching land.

An ant's sense of smell is as good as a dog's.

 A tortoise called Speedy was once found by police on the fast lane of the M6 motorway! Since a lot of people said Speedy was theirs, the police set up an identity parade of six tortoises to find the real owner.

 The Canary Islands were not named after the bird, but after wild dogs once found there. *Canariae insulae* means 'island of dogs'.

 The kangaroo cannot jump if its tail is lifted off the ground.

 The silkworm is not a worm, it is a caterpillar.

Some animals may not be as dead as they seem. An Egyptian snail was thought quite dead when it went on show on an ancient Egyptian tablet in the British Museum in 1846. Two years later, to everyone's surprise, the snail came back to life. It began to repair its shell and went on to live for some time.

Crocodiles grow from eggs. The strange thing is, when the baby crocodiles hatch they are three times as big as the egg they come out of!

 A horned toad is not a toad, it is a lizard.

During the First World War, travel between Britain and France was limited. One of the oddest journeys was made by a shrew. London Zoo didn't have one, and heard of a shrew called Albert who was kept by British soldiers in France. So, a soldier was given emergency leave to take Albert to London Zoo. It was quite a job, since Albert needed to be fed on beef every two hours of the 24-hour journey.

 A guinea pig is not a pig, it is a rodent.

 There are many freaks in nature. One which can be seen in Britain is winged cats. Six have been found in the last 100 years, one being found in Wales in 1985. The wings are strips of fur-covered skin that grow from the shoulder to the middle of the body when the cat is about four years old. The Welsh cat had an 18-cm wing-span, and seemed to use the wings to help it jump.

In Africa, elephants discovered a sort of penicillin before people. Sick elephants were seen using a type of slimy mould for wounds and drank it to make them better. Local native people saw this and began using the slime for their own cuts and sores.

 In 1973 a cat called Whisky was left by accident in Cambridge. He made his way to his home in West Yorkshire in the next 25 days, covering a distance of 150 miles.

 Female armadillos always have four babies at a time and they are always either all male or all female.

 A kangaroo can hop at up to 40 miles an hour.

 A frog has to close its eyes to swallow.

 Pigs can run a 7.5-minute mile.

In the USA during the Second World War, there was a plan to use millions of bats to drop firebombs on Germany and Japan. The idea of the "bat bomb" began in 1942. Up to 30 million bats were to be trained for the mission. After some time, small bombs were made and tied on to the chests of the first bats with string. The idea was that as the bats began to fly, they would chew the string until the bombs dropped off on to the ground below. The bats were kept cool so they would go to sleep until they were needed. Unfortunately, some of the bats stayed asleep for longer than was expected, others flew away as soon as their cages were open and some, still dozy, just fell to the ground. In one trial, a bat bomb mission escaped on a US airfield and their bombs burned down a hangar and set fire to a general's car. After more trials, the idea of the bat bomb finally worked. The only problem was that by then the war was over.

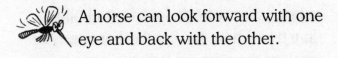 A horse can look forward with one eye and back with the other.

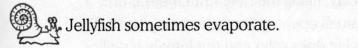 Jellyfish sometimes evaporate.

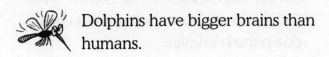 Dolphins have bigger brains than humans.

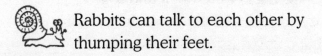 Rabbits can talk to each other by thumping their feet.

The hornbill bird has very odd behaviour when nesting. The female bird, which has a large clumsy beak, looks for a hollow in a tree where she can lay her eggs. As soon as the eggs are laid, the male starts filling up the hole. He brings in damp clay, filling the hole until there is only a small opening for the female's beak. The clay dries solid and the female is walled in until the eggs hatch. The male feeds her through the gap which is left. When the chicks are born, both parents break down the hard wall.

Beavers can swim underwater without taking a breath for 15 minutes.

Llamas have extremely bad breath.

In the 1700s a trapper could sell the deerskin of a buck for a dollar, which is why dollars are known as bucks.

Swordfish can reach speeds of 60 miles an hour.

 Fish can become seasick if they are kept aboard a ship too long.

 A flea can jump more than 30 cm.

 As you might guess, giraffes often have throat infections.

 A giraffe needs a big heart to pump the blood up its long neck. The average size of its heart is 60 cm.

 The shell of an egg is normally 12%, or one eighth, of its weight.

The egg of the kiwi is one quarter of its mother's size!

 Parrots are very good at hearing – during the First World War a group of parrots were kept at the top of the Eiffel Tower in Paris. They were listening out for planes.

 Earthworms do not have eyes or ears.

 Giraffes cannot swim, elephants can.

 Cats cannot taste sweet things.

 Fish have no eyelids; their eyes are always open.

A termite can live for 30 years.

 Baboons cannot throw overarm.

 An electric eel will short-circuit if it is put in salt, rather than fresh, water.

 The edible dormouse of Europe can hibernate for up to six months a year.

 A duck will often swim while sleeping.

 A pigeon's feathers weigh more than its bones.

 Birds cannot sweat.

The ancient Egyptians wrapped dead crocodiles in paper. A lot of the paper had writing on it, and when read, has been important in finding out how the ancient Egyptians lived.

 All polar bears are left-handed. Polar bear mothers usually have twins. They are the size of rats when born and are blind for a month.

 Dog sleds delivered the post in Alaska until 1963.

 After mating, the female praying mantis kills and eats the male.

The vampire bat is the most dangerous of all bats. This is not only because they bite animals and suck their blood. It is because they can spread disease which can kill other animals and birds. One bat was once seen which had taken in so much blood it could not fly.

 The whale shark has the thickest skin of any animal. It can be between 10 and 20 cm thick on a grown adult. When attacked, it can tighten its skin so it becomes like iron. It is like a solid shield, which hardly anything can get through.

 Telephone poles in Uganda and Kenya are higher than in the rest of the world so that giraffes can walk under the wires.

 A newborn panda is smaller than a mouse.

In a test alongside a car in the United States in 1941, a pronghorn antelope was able to run at 35 miles an hour for almost four miles without tiring.

 Cows can be identified by their noseprints.

 A giraffe has a 40-cm-long tongue.

 Cats, camels and giraffes move their front and hind legs on one side, then front and hind legs on the other as they walk.

 A rattlesnake can bite you up to half an hour after it is dead.